The Numb

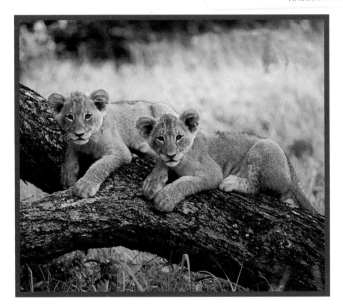

Adria Klein

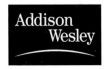

Toronto

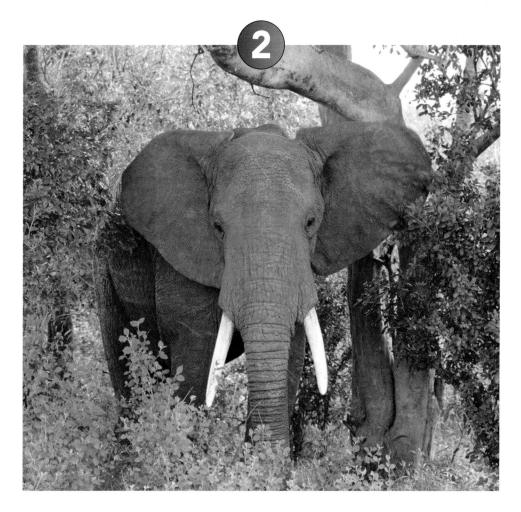

Look at my two grey ears.

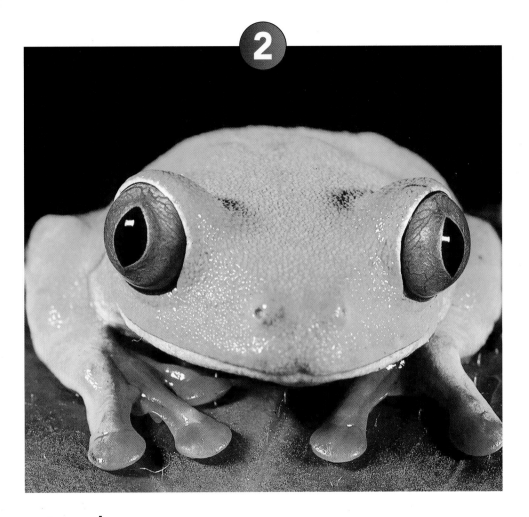

Look at my two orange eyes.

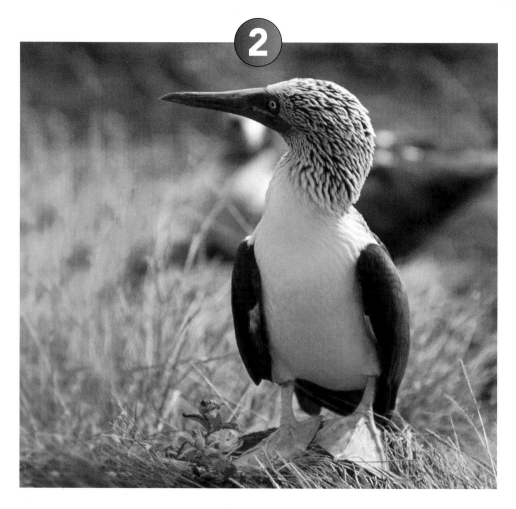

Look at my two blue feet.

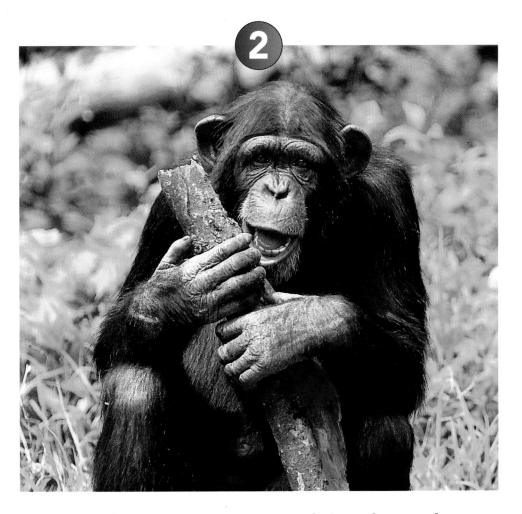

Look at my two big hands.

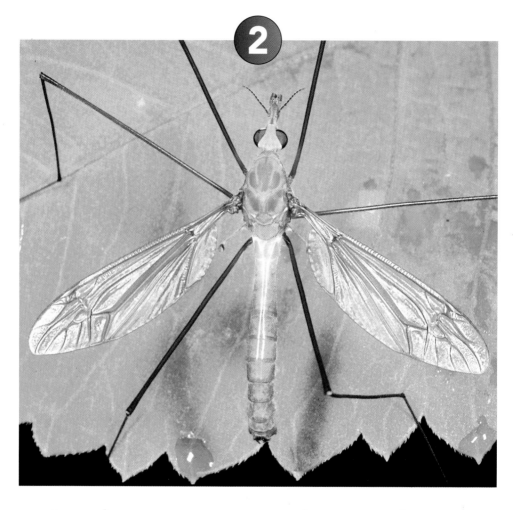

Look at my two long wings.

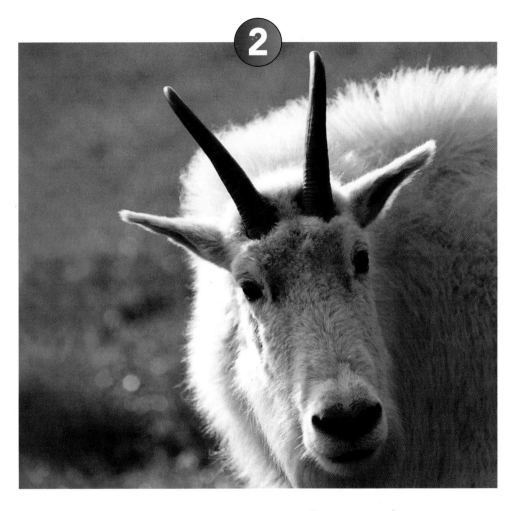

Look at my two sharp horns.

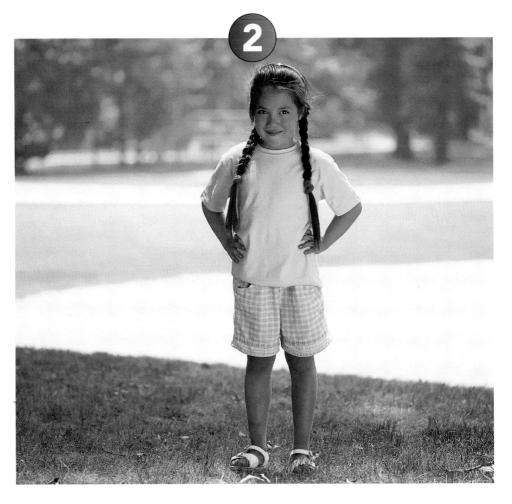

What do you have two of?